Tunes for Teens from Musicals

...CES
AND ACCOMPANIMENTS

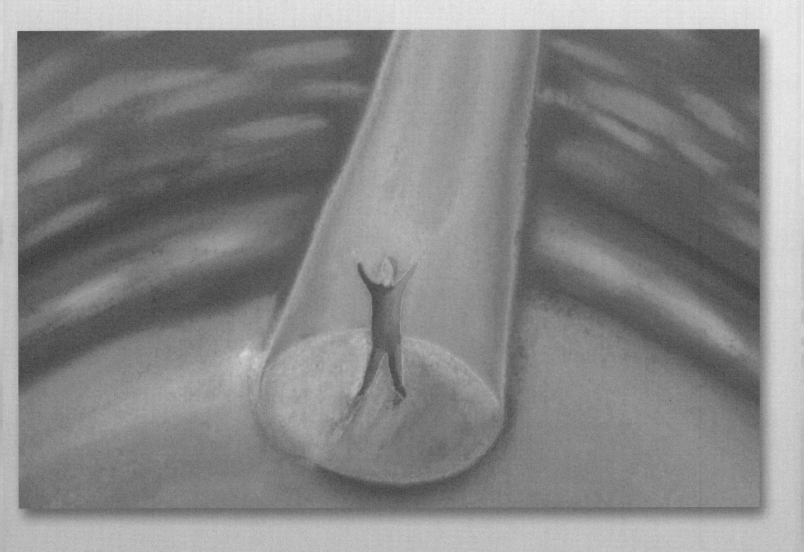

ISBN 0-634-08409-7

HAL•LEONARD® CORPORATION

7777 W. BLUEMOUND RD. P.O. BOX 13819 MILWAUKEE, WI 53213

Visit Hal Leonard Online at
www.halleonard.com

Contents

Vocal tracks produced by:
Michael Dansicker

Pianists on the CD:
Michael Dansicker (tracks 2, 3, 5, 8, 12, 13, 15, 18)
Brian Dean (tracks 4, 14)
Christopher Ruck (tracks 1, 6, 7, 9-11, 16, 17, 19, 20)

COMEDY TONIGHT

from *A Funny Thing Happened on the Way to the Forum*

Words and Music by
Stephen Sondheim

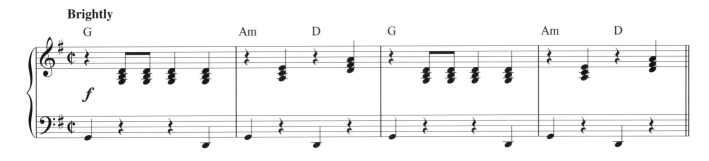

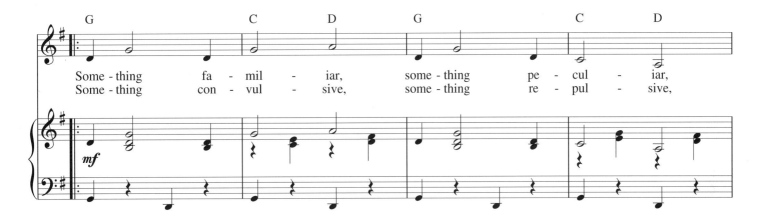

Some-thing fa-mil-iar, some-thing pe-cul-iar,
Some-thing con-vul-sive, some-thing re-pul-sive,

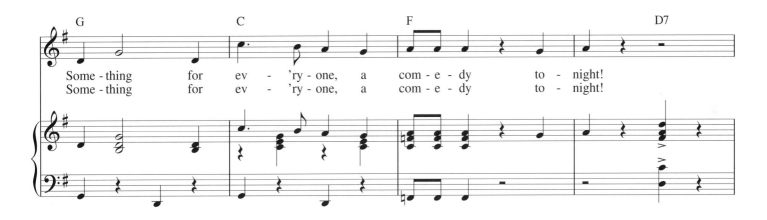

Some-thing for ev-'ry-one, a com-e-dy to-night!
Some-thing for ev-'ry-one, a com-e-dy to-night!

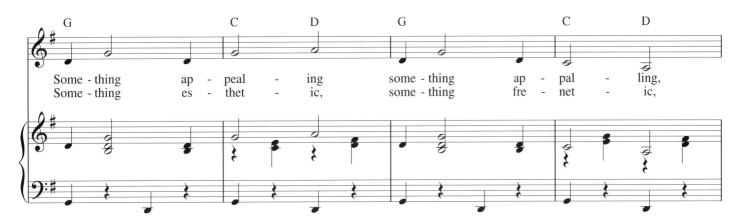

Some-thing ap-peal-ing some-thing ap-pal-ling,
Some-thing es-thet-ic, some-thing fre-net-ic,

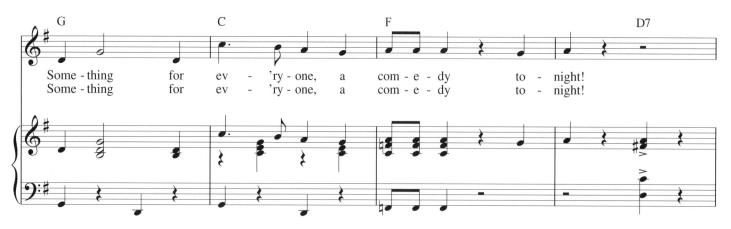

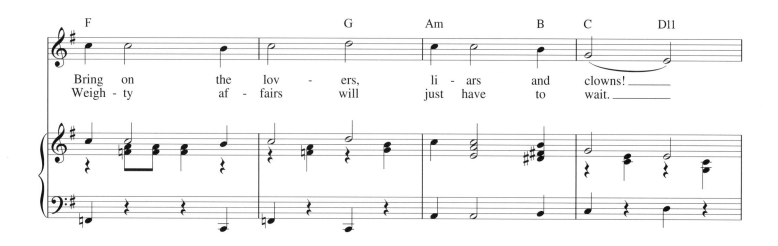

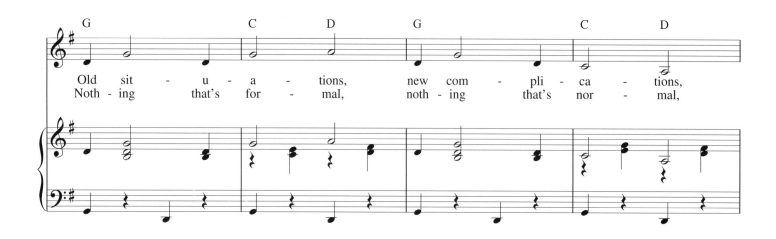

ALL I NEED IS THE GIRL

from *Gypsy*

Words by Stephen Sondheim
Music by Jule Styne

Moderately, in 2

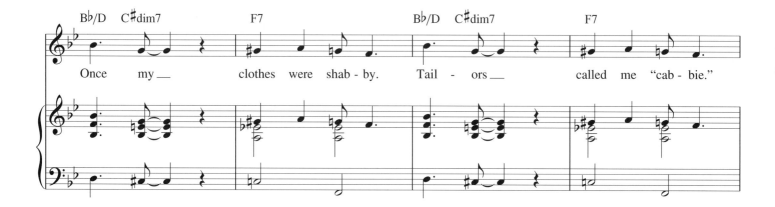

Once my — clothes were shab-by. Tail-ors — called me "cab-bie."

So I — took a vow, — said, "This bum-'ll be beau Brum-mell."

Now I'm — smooth and snap-py. Now my — tail-or's hap-py.

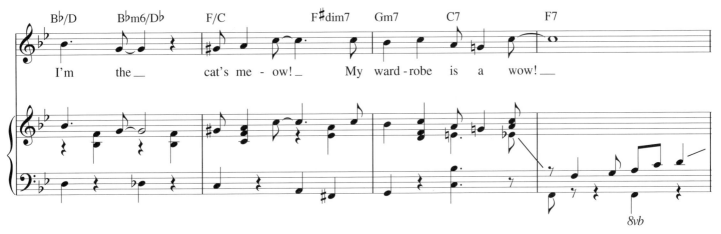

I'm the __ cat's me - ow! __ My ward-robe is a wow! __

Par - is __ silk, __ Har - ris __ tweed. __

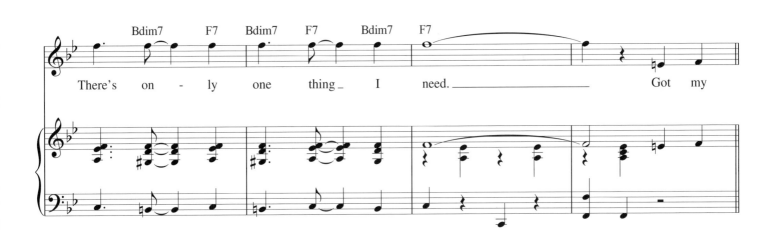

There's on - ly one thing __ I need. _____ Got my

tweed pressed, __ got my best vest. __ All I

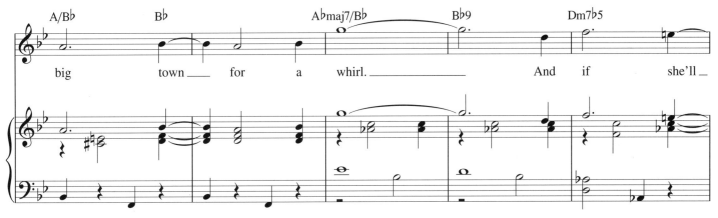

big town ____ for a whirl. _____ And if she'll ____

____ say, "My dar - ling, I'm yours," I'll throw ____ a - way ____ my striped tie ____

____ and my best pressed tweed. ____ All I real - ly need ____

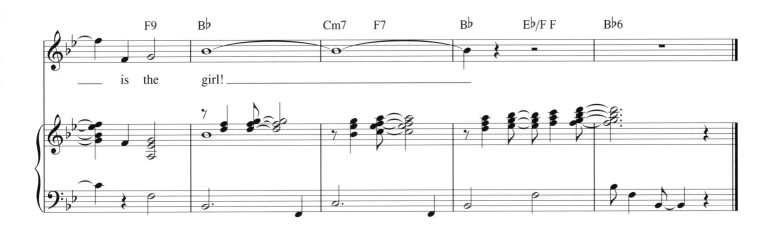

____ is the girl! _____

MY DEFENSES ARE DOWN

from the Stage Production
Annie Get Your Gun

Music and Words by
Irving Berlin

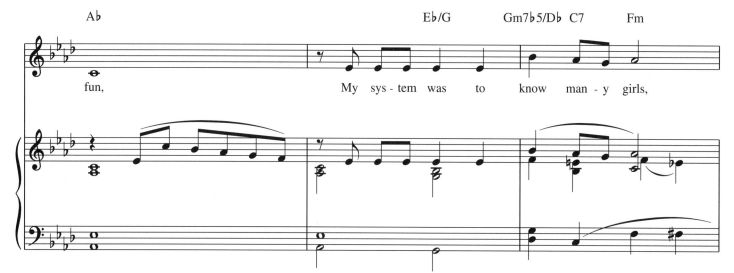

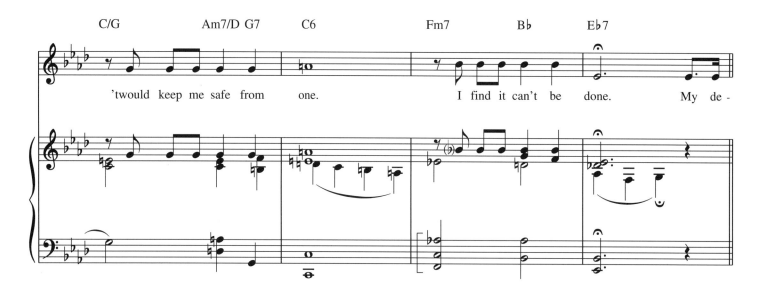

Moderato

fen - ses are down, __ she's bro - ken my re - sis - tance and I don't know where I

am. I went in - to the fight like a li - on, but I

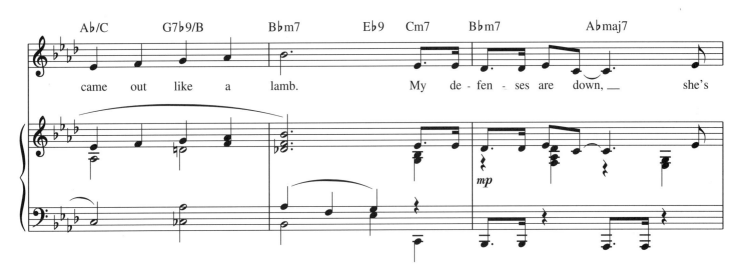

came out like a lamb. My de - fen - ses are down, __ she's

got me where she wants me, and I can't es - cape no - how. I could

speak to my heart when it weak - ened, but my heart won't lis - ten now.

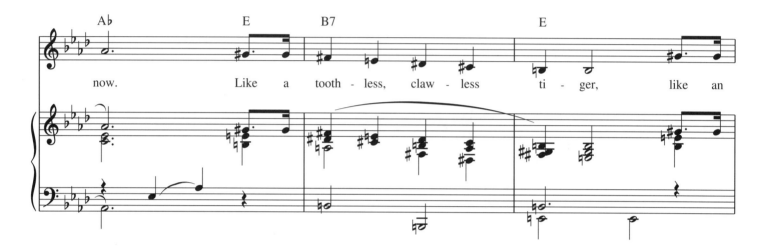

Like a tooth - less, claw - less ti - ger, like an

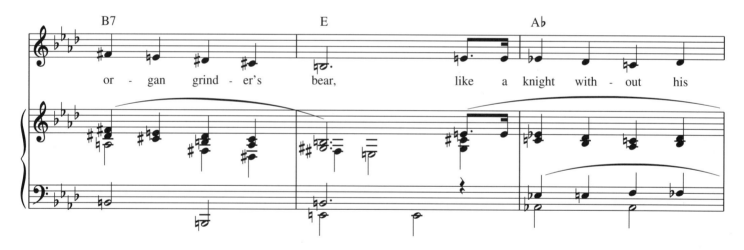

or - gan grind - er's bear, like a knight with - out his

ar - mor, like Sam - son ____ with - out his hair. My de -

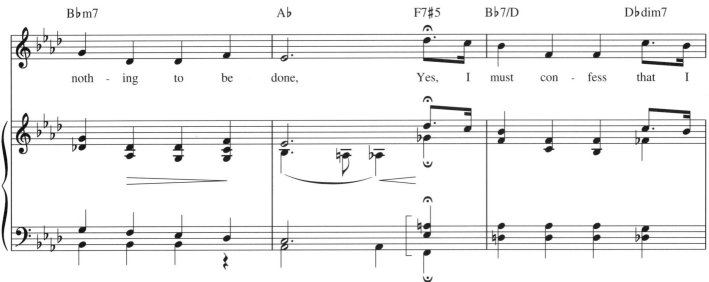

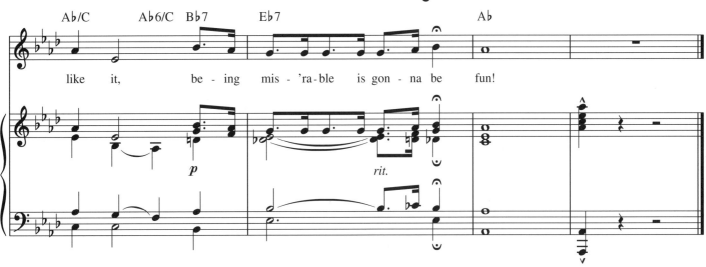

GONNA BUILD A MOUNTAIN

from the Musical Production *Stop the World - I Want to Get Off*

Words and Music by Leslie Bricusse
and Anthony Newley

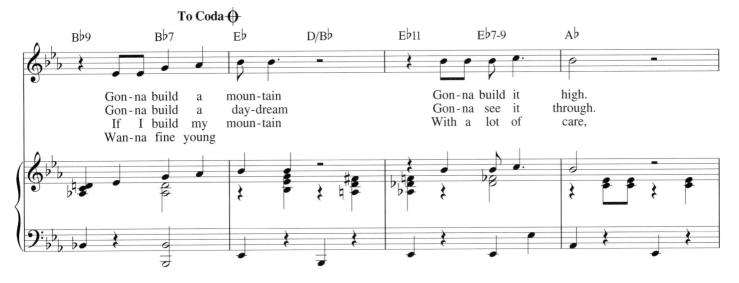

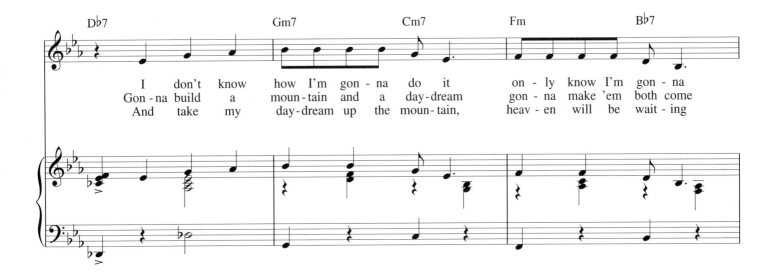

CODA

son
son

to take my place
to take my place

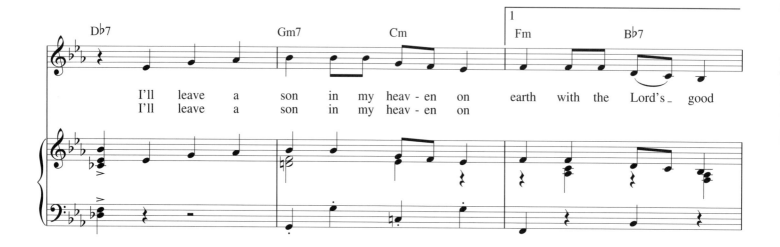

I'll leave a son in my heav-en on earth with the Lord's_ good
I'll leave a son in my heav-en on

grace.

With a fine young earth with the good Lord's

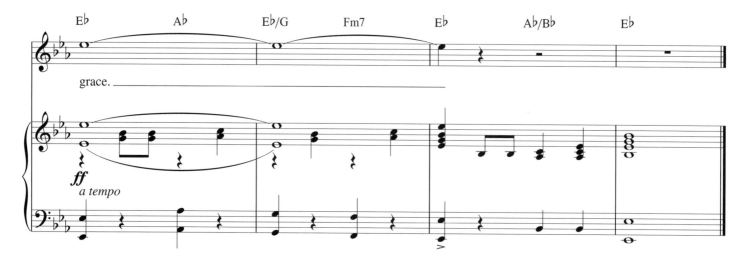

grace.____

LES POISSONS
from Walt Disney's *The Little Mermaid*

Lyrics by Howard Ashman
Music by Alan Menken

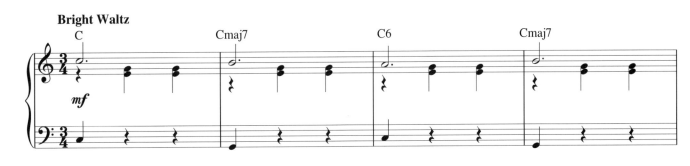

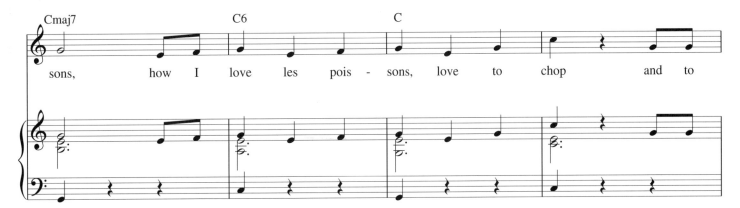

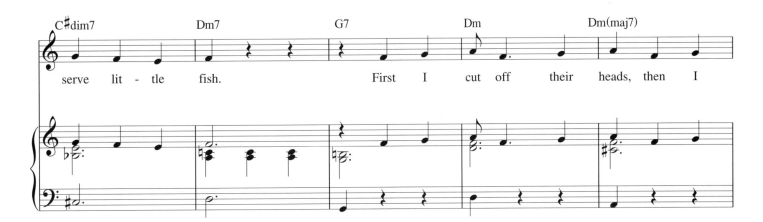

pull out their bones. Ah mais oui, ca c'est tou - jours de - lish.

Les pois - sons, les pois - sons, hee hee hee, ____ hah hah hah. ____

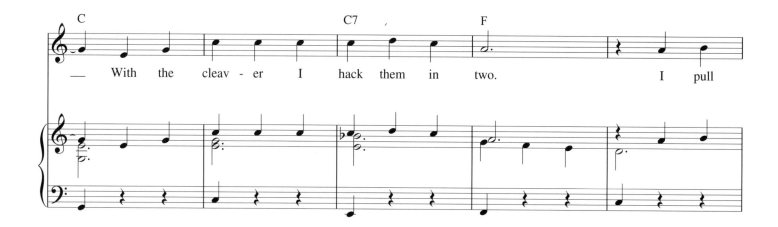

____ With the cleav - er I hack them in two. I pull

out what's in - side and I serve it up fried. God, I

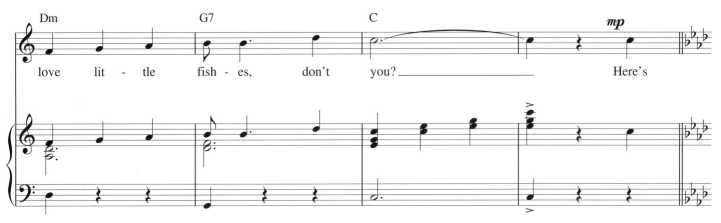

love lit - tle fish - es, don't you?_____ Here's

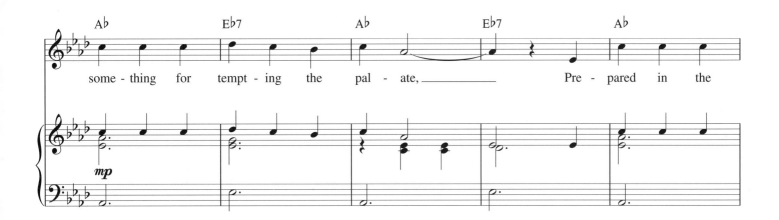

some - thing for tempt - ing the pal - ate,_____ Pre - pared in the

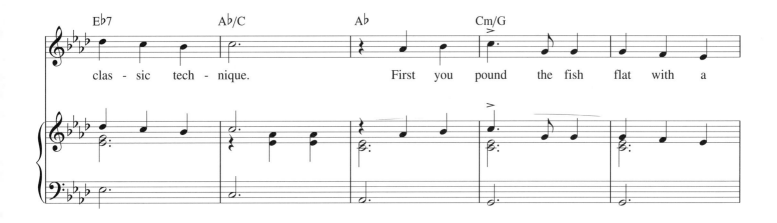

clas - sic tech - nique. First you pound the fish flat with a

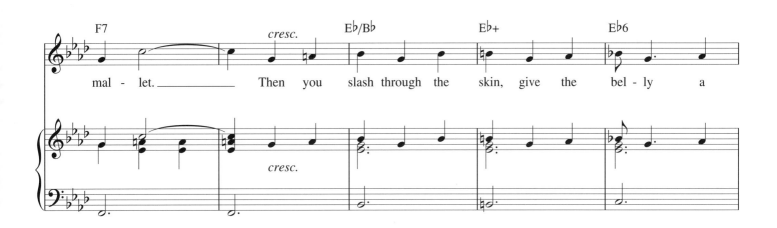

mal - let._____ Then you slash through the skin, give the bel - ly a

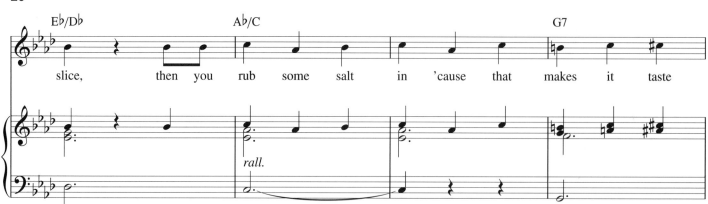

slice, then you rub some salt in 'cause that makes it taste

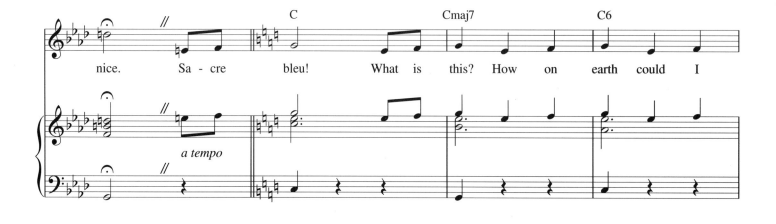

nice. Sa - cre bleu! What is this? How on earth could I

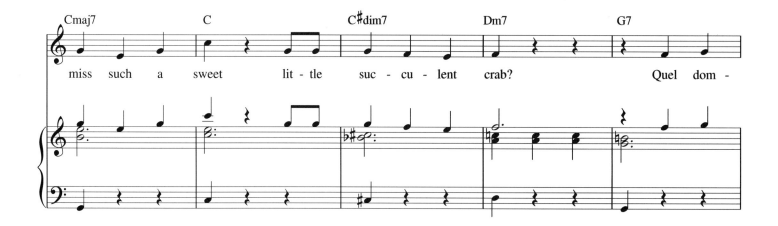

miss such a sweet lit - tle suc - cu - lent crab? Quel dom -

mage. What a loss. Here we go in the sauce. Now some

flour ___ I think, just a dab. Now I stuff you with

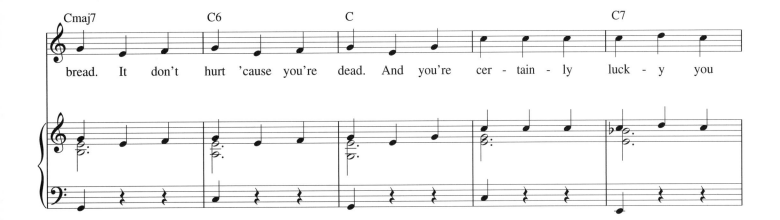

bread. It don't hurt 'cause you're dead. And you're cer - tain - ly luck - y you

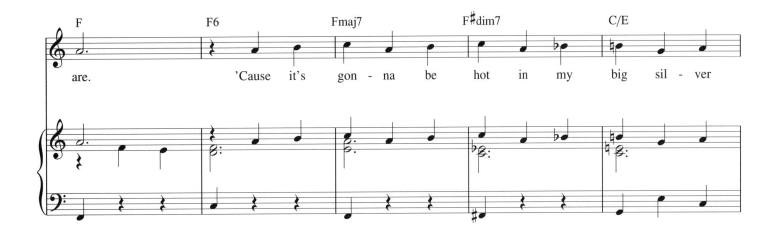

are. 'Cause it's gon - na be hot in my big sil - ver

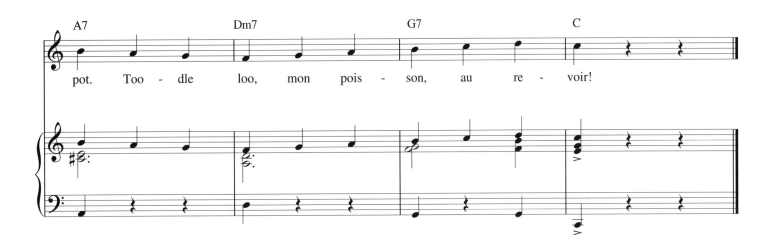

pot. Too - dle loo, mon pois - son, au re - voir!

PUTTIN' ON THE RITZ
from the Motion Picture *Puttin' on the Ritz*

Words and Music by
Irving Berlin

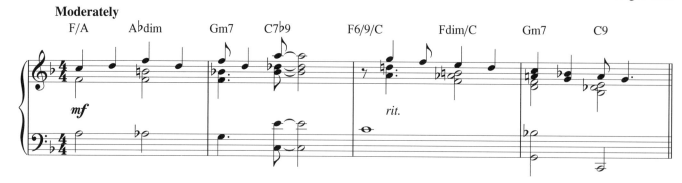

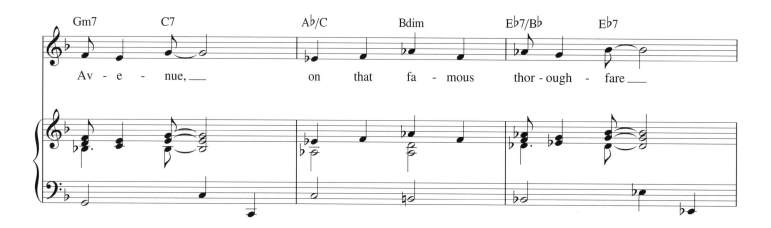

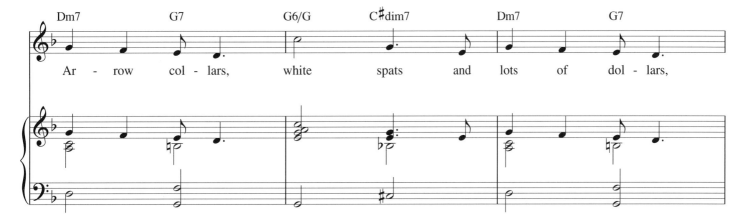

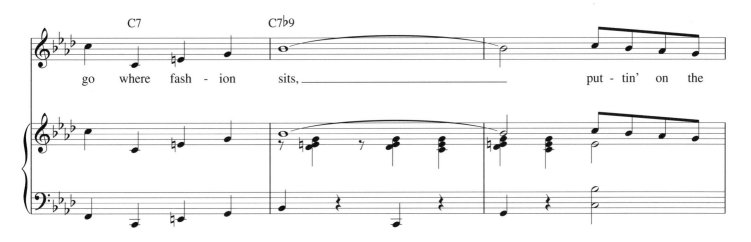

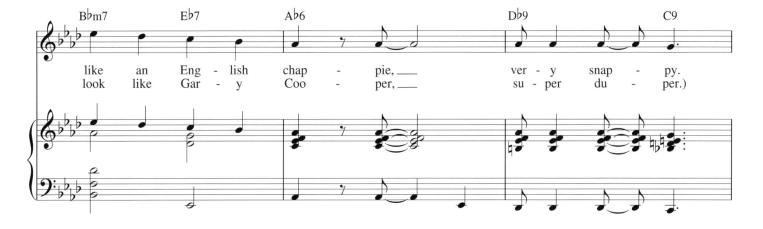

like an Eng - lish chap - pie, _____ ver - y snap - py.
look like Gar - y Coo - per, _____ su - per du - per.)

Come, let's mix where Rock - e - fel - lers walk with sticks or "um - ber-

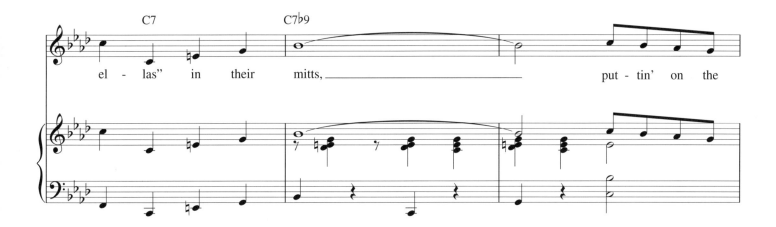

el - las" in their mitts, _____ put - tin' on the

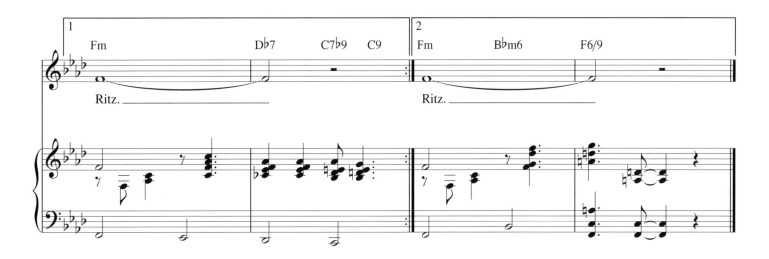

Ritz. _____

Ritz. _____

SOON IT'S GONNA RAIN

from *The Fantasticks*

Words by Tom Jones
Music by Harvey Schmidt

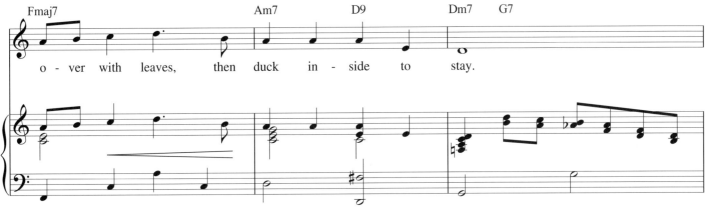

Then we'll let it rain. We'll not feel it. Then we'll let it rain,

rain pell mell. And we'll not com-plain if it nev - er stops at

all. _____ We'll live and love with - in our own four

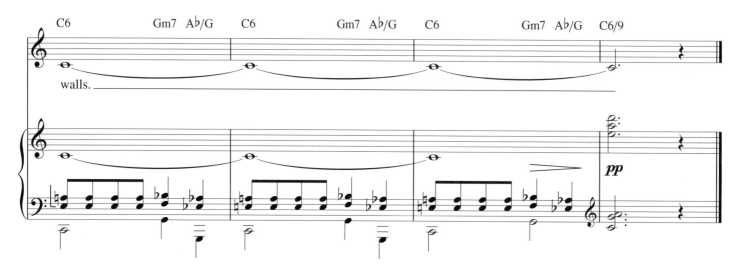

walls. _____

WHEN I'M NOT NEAR THE GIRL I LOVE

from *Finian's Rainbow*

Words by E.Y. Harburg
Music by Burton Lane

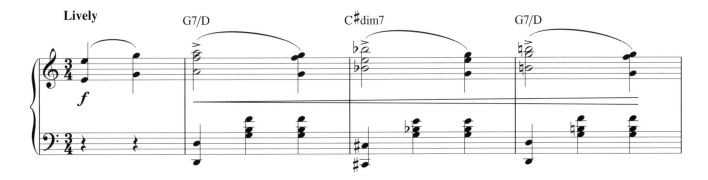

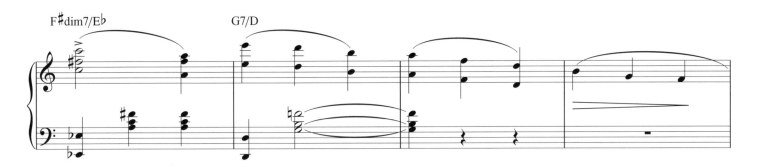

Oh my heart is beat - ing wild - ly _____
(D.S.) fess - ing a con - fess - ion _____

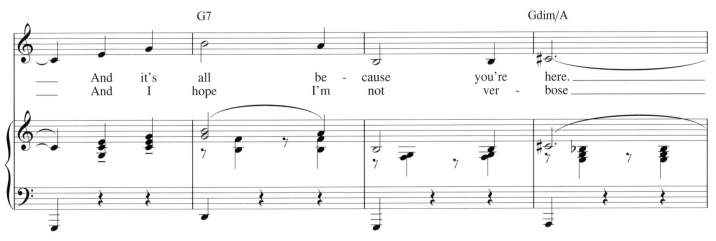

_____ And it's all be - cause you're here. _____
_____ And I hope I'm not ver - bose _____

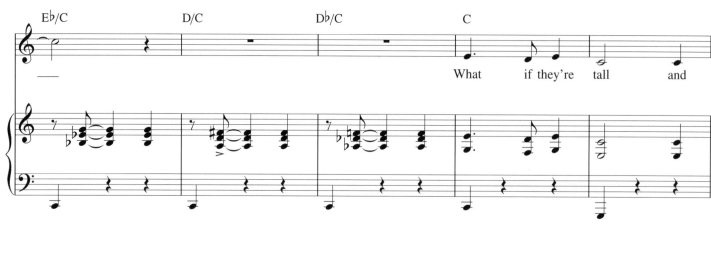

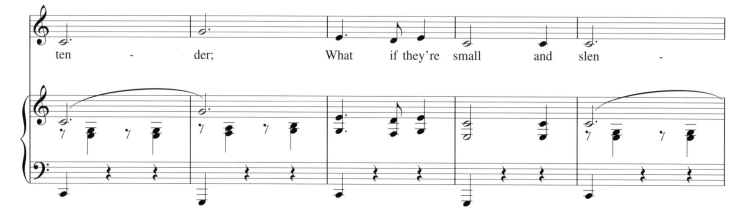

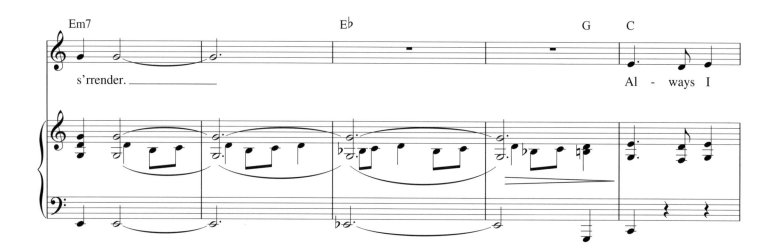

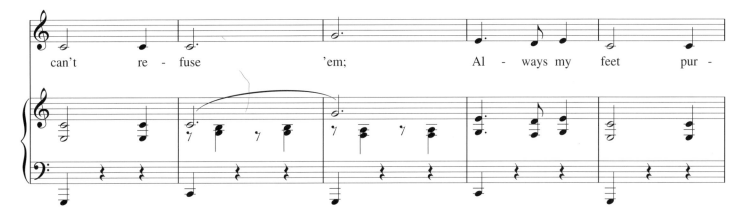

can't re - fuse 'em; Al - ways my feet pur -

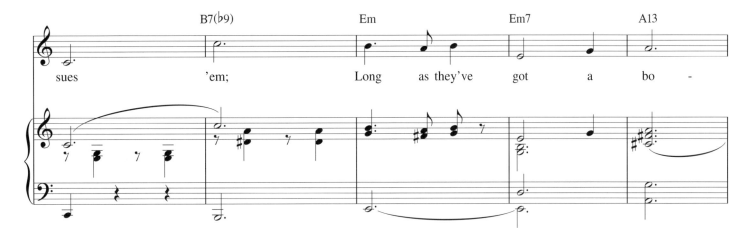

B7(♭9) Em Em7 A13

sues 'em; Long as they've got a bo -

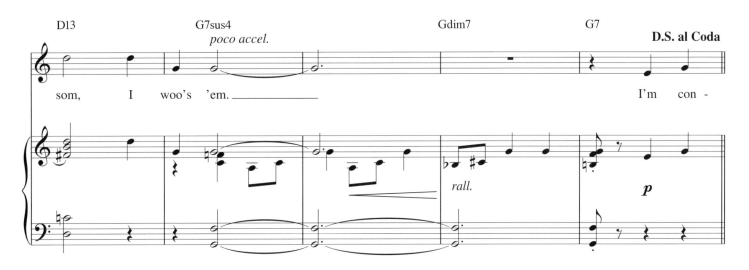

D13 G7sus4 Gdim7 G7 **D.S. al Coda**

poco accel.

som, I woo's 'em. I'm con -

rall.

p

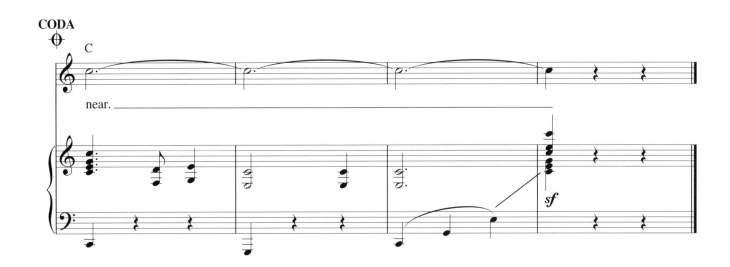

CODA

C

near.

sf

WAITIN' FOR THE LIGHT TO SHINE

from *Big River*

Words and Music by
Roger Miller

A WONDERFUL DAY LIKE TODAY

from
*The Roar of the Greasepaint—
The Smell of the Crowd*

Words and Music by Leslie Bricusse
and Anthony Newley

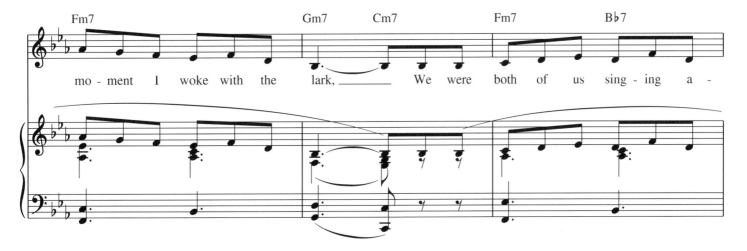

mo - ment I woke with the lark, _____ We were both of us sing - ing a -

way. _____ And the sky was so blue, I in - stinc - tive - ly knew We were

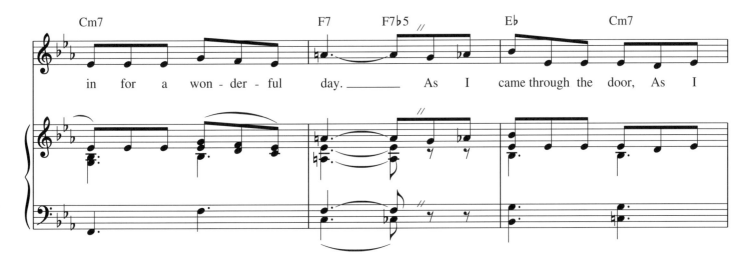

in for a won - der - ful day. _____ As I came through the door, As I

Chorus - Brightly

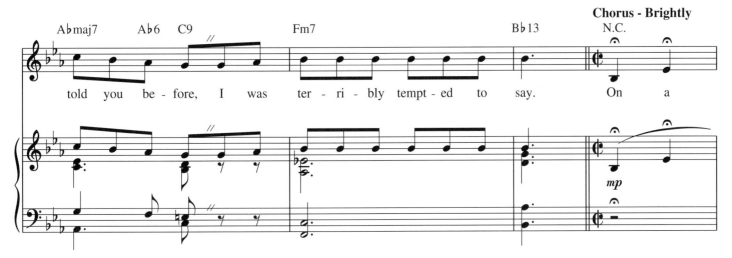

told you be - fore, I was ter - ri - bly tempt - ed to say. On a

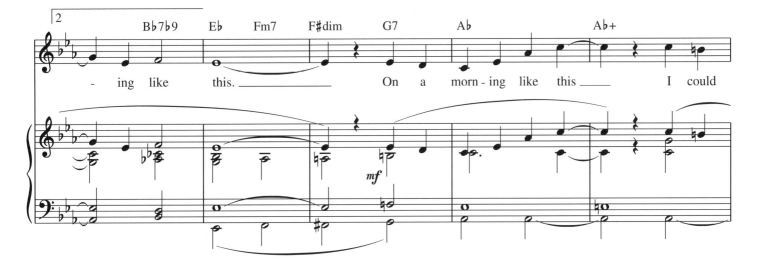

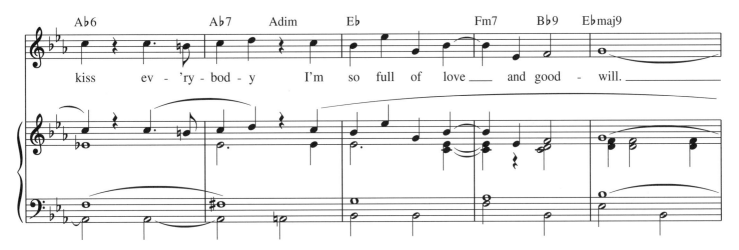

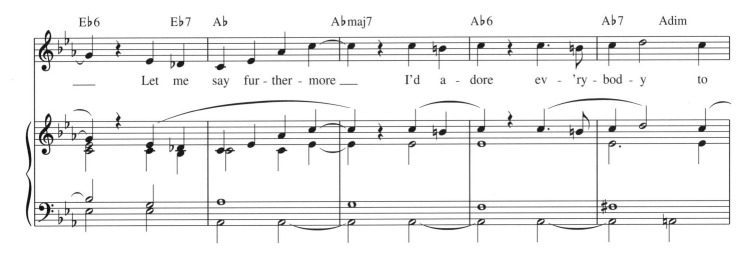

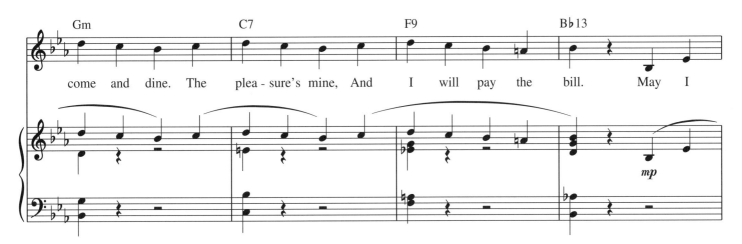

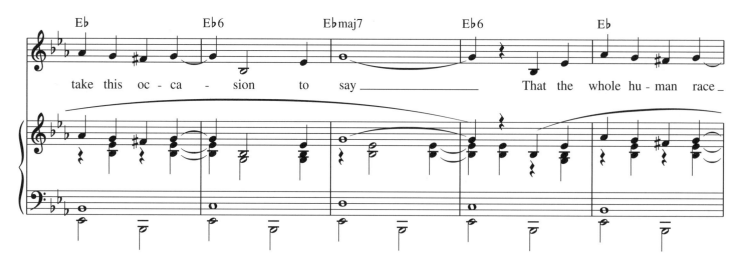

take this oc - ca - sion to say ____ That the whole hu - man race ____

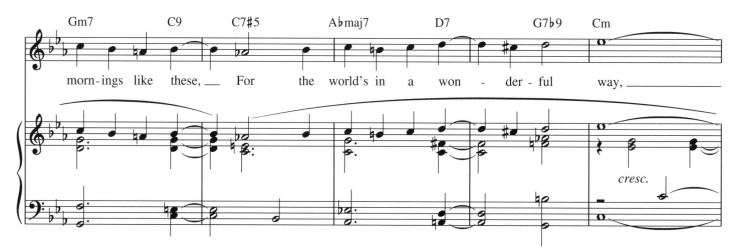

____ should go down on its knees, ____ Show that we're grate - ful for

morn - ings like these, ____ For the world's in a won - der - ful way, ____

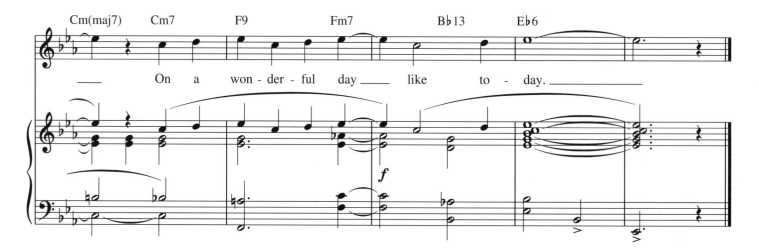

____ On a won - der - ful day ____ like to - day. ____